National Parks

2025 PLANNER

JULY 2024–DECEMBER 2025

ROCK
POINT

2025 YEAR AT A GLANCE

JANUARY

S	M	T	W	T	F	S
			1	2	3	4
5	6	7	8	9	10	11
12	13	14	15	16	17	18
19	20	21	22	23	24	25
26	27	28	29	30	31	

FEBRUARY

S	M	T	W	T	F	S
						1
2	3	4	5	6	7	8
9	10	11	12	13	14	15
16	17	18	19	20	21	22
23	24	25	26	27	28	

MARCH

S	M	T	W	T	F	S
						1
2	3	4	5	6	7	8
9	10	11	12	13	14	15
16	17	18	19	20	21	22
23	24	25	26	27	28	29
30	31					

APRIL

S	M	T	W	T	F	S
		1	2	3	4	5
6	7	8	9	10	11	12
13	14	15	16	17	18	19
20	21	22	23	24	25	26
27	28	29	30			

MAY

S	M	T	W	T	F	S
				1	2	3
4	5	6	7	8	9	10
11	12	13	14	15	16	17
18	19	20	21	22	23	24
25	26	27	28	29	30	31

JUNE

S	M	T	W	T	F	S
1	2	3	4	5	6	7
8	9	10	11	12	13	14
15	16	17	18	19	20	21
22	23	24	25	26	27	28
29	30					

JULY

S	M	T	W	T	F	S
		1	2	3	4	5
6	7	8	9	10	11	12
13	14	15	16	17	18	19
20	21	22	23	24	25	26
27	28	29	30	31		

AUGUST

S	M	T	W	T	F	S
					1	2
3	4	5	6	7	8	9
10	11	12	13	14	15	16
17	18	19	20	21	22	23
24	25	26	27	28	29	30
31						

SEPTEMBER

S	M	T	W	T	F	S
	1	2	3	4	5	6
7	8	9	10	11	12	13
14	15	16	17	18	19	20
21	22	23	24	25	26	27
28	29	30				

OCTOBER

S	M	T	W	T	F	S
			1	2	3	4
5	6	7	8	9	10	11
12	13	14	15	16	17	18
19	20	21	22	23	24	25
26	27	28	29	30	31	

NOVEMBER

S	M	T	W	T	F	S
						1
2	3	4	5	6	7	8
9	10	11	12	13	14	15
16	17	18	19	20	21	22
23	24	25	26	27	28	29
30						

DECEMBER

S	M	T	W	T	F	S
	1	2	3	4	5	6
7	8	9	10	11	12	13
14	15	16	17	18	19	20
21	22	23	24	25	26	27
28	29	30	31			

2026 YEAR AT A GLANCE

JANUARY

S	M	T	W	T	F	S
				1	2	3
4	5	6	7	8	9	10
11	12	13	14	15	16	17
18	19	20	21	22	23	24
25	26	27	28	29	30	31

FEBRUARY

S	M	T	W	T	F	S
1	2	3	4	5	6	7
8	9	10	11	12	13	14
15	16	17	18	19	20	21
22	23	24	25	26	27	28

MARCH

S	M	T	W	T	F	S
1	2	3	4	5	6	7
8	9	10	11	12	13	14
15	16	17	18	19	20	21
22	23	24	25	26	27	28
29	30	31				

APRIL

S	M	T	W	T	F	S
			1	2	3	4
5	6	7	8	9	10	11
12	13	14	15	16	17	18
19	20	21	22	23	24	25
26	27	28	29	30		

MAY

S	M	T	W	T	F	S
					1	2
3	4	5	6	7	8	9
10	11	12	13	14	15	16
17	18	19	20	21	22	23
24	25	26	27	28	29	30
31						

JUNE

S	M	T	W	T	F	S
	1	2	3	4	5	6
7	8	9	10	11	12	13
14	15	16	17	18	19	20
21	22	23	24	25	26	27
28	29	30				

JULY

S	M	T	W	T	F	S
			1	2	3	4
5	6	7	8	9	10	11
12	13	14	15	16	17	18
19	20	21	22	23	24	25
26	27	28	29	30	31	

AUGUST

S	M	T	W	T	F	S
						1
2	3	4	5	6	7	8
9	10	11	12	13	14	15
16	17	18	19	20	21	22
23	24	25	26	27	28	29
30	31					

SEPTEMBER

S	M	T	W	T	F	S
		1	2	3	4	5
6	7	8	9	10	11	12
13	14	15	16	17	18	19
20	21	22	23	24	25	26
27	28	29	30			

OCTOBER

S	M	T	W	T	F	S
				1	2	3
4	5	6	7	8	9	10
11	12	13	14	15	16	17
18	19	20	21	22	23	24
25	26	27	28	29	30	31

NOVEMBER

S	M	T	W	T	F	S
1	2	3	4	5	6	7
8	9	10	11	12	13	14
15	16	17	18	19	20	21
22	23	24	25	26	27	28
29	30					

DECEMBER

S	M	T	W	T	F	S
		1	2	3	4	5
6	7	8	9	10	11	12
13	14	15	16	17	18	19
20	21	22	23	24	25	26
27	28	29	30	31		

JULY
Indiana Dunes National Park

In 2019, the Indiana Dunes National Park, previously known as the Indiana Dunes National Lakeshore, was redesignated as the nation's 61st National Park. The Wisconsin Glacier melting into Lake Michigan, the fifth largest freshwater lake in the world, deserves our thanks for leaving behind a variety of different natural landscapes, including the dune ridgeline. Along 15 miles of the coastline is where the state's most ecologically diverse area begins. Covered in native flora and wild lupines, the Indiana Dunes National Park is the best place to spot hundreds of migratory birds and explore unique sandy beaches with shifting sands of quartz

and silica. For every hiker or nature explorer, hike over 50 miles of trails where the Kankakee River winds through thriving regions of sandy soil and black oak savannas. Visit the quiet woodlands and sunny prairies where you might encounter sightings of wildlife living and feeding. Find family-friendly fun among nature's discoveries with leftover historic debris of the glacial moraines, or reserve a table for the whole family in one of the covered picnic shelters. Open year-round, Indiana Dunes National Park offers limitless attractions and recreations along the Indiana coast, with much more to discover during the winter months.

JULY 2024

NOTES	SUNDAY	MONDAY	TUESDAY
		1	2
		CANADA DAY (CAN)	
	7	8	9
	14	15	16
●	21	22	23
	28	29	30

JULY 2024

WEDNESDAY	THURSDAY	FRIDAY	SATURDAY
3	4 ○	5	6
	INDEPENDENCE DAY (US)		
10	11	12 ☽	13
17	18	19	20
24	25	26 ☾	27
31			

INDIANA DUNES NATIONAL PARK

LOCATION: Northwestern Indiana

SIZE: 15,000 acres

BEST TIME TO VISIT: April through October

FAUNA & FLORA: With more than 350 species living or migrating through the area, witness thousands of Sandhill Cranes and hundreds of hawks—in the winter see wood frogs, Dark-eyed Junco, and Snowy Owls—as well as approximately 1,130 native vascular plants.

ENDANGERED FAUNA & FLORA: Home to populations of 30% of Indiana's rare, endangered, and special concern plant species, including Pitcher's thistle.

MAIN ATTRACTIONS: On the Indiana National Lakeshore is one of the world's largest lakeshore dunes, Mount Baldy, a 125-foot "living dune" shaped by glacial sands. Enjoy swimming, paddling, camping, fishing, and horseback riding in the summer; and skiing, snowshoeing, and hiking in the winter.

PRIMARY PURPOSE: To preserve, restore, and protect the outstanding ecological and biological diversity and geological features of the southern shore of Lake Michigan.

JULY

MONDAY CANADA DAY (CAN)   **1**

TUESDAY   **2**

WEDNESDAY   **3**

THURSDAY INDEPENDENCE DAY (US)   **4**

FRIDAY ○   **5**

SATURDAY   **6**

SUNDAY   **7**

JULY 2024

MONDAY 8

TUESDAY 9

WEDNESDAY 10

THURSDAY 11

FRIDAY   **12**

SATURDAY◗   **13**

SUNDAY   **14**

The Indiana Dunes landscape contains disjunct
flora, boreal forest remnants, and species with Atlantic
coast affinities.

JULY 2024

MONDAY   **15**

TUESDAY   **16**

WEDNESDAY   **17**

THURSDAY   **18**

FRIDAY **19**

SATURDAY **20**

SUNDAY ● **21**

Visit over 60 historic structures in the park, including a National Historic Landmark, the Bailly Homestead.

JULY 2024

MONDAY   **22**

TUESDAY   **23**

WEDNESDAY   **24**

THURSDAY   **25**

FRIDAY   **26**

SATURDAY ◖   **27**

SUNDAY   **28**

Climb Diana's Dune and get a boundless vantage point where you can see 36 miles into the distance to Chicago.

AUGUST
Rocky Mountain National Park

Consider Rocky Mountain a jack-of-all-trades. Thanks to the Great Continental Divide running through them, they are one of the most ecologically and climatically diverse of all the U.S. National Parks. The Rocky Mountain Park Act signed by Woodrow Wilson in 1915 established the park we know today, often referred to as a Land of Extremes. With a drier, glacial east side and a lusher, forest-filled west, Rocky Mountain National Park offers a range of wonderful natural sights to see—from blooming meadows to glistening alpine lakes to towering mountain peaks. The first people here were Paleo Indians as far back as 11,000 years ago,

who traveled along Trail Ridge Road to hunt for bison and mammoth. Rewind the clock with a colorful drive down that same path where today you will find bighorn sheep, marmots, pikas, and 200 species of alpine plants. Experienced climbers and mountaineers can climb and cross vertical rock faces to the park's tallest mountain, Longs Peak, with 20 more climbs reaching above 13,000 feet. Looking for a less strenuous adventure? Bring a picnic basket to Bear Lake and admire the view formed during the ice age or pitch a tent at a campground and spend the night. The possibilities are as eclectic as the Rocky Mountains themselves.

AUGUST 2024

NOTES	SUNDAY	MONDAY	TUESDAY
○	4	5	6
		SUMMER BANK HOLIDAY (UK-SCT)	
	11 ◗	12	13
	18 ●	19	20
	25 ◖	26	27
		SUMMER BANK HOLIDAY (UK-ENG/NIR/WAL)	

AUGUST 2024

WEDNESDAY	THURSDAY	FRIDAY	SATURDAY
	1	2	3
7	8	9	10
14	15	16	17
21	22	23	24
28	29	30	31

ROCKY MOUNTAIN NATIONAL PARK

LOCATION: Northern Colorado

SIZE: 265,000 acres

BEST TIME TO VISIT: November through April

FAUNA & FLORA: Discover 900 species of plants around the park. At high altitudes find a unique assortment of wildlife, including marmots and pikas. At lower altitudes find bighorn sheep, deer, coyotes, and the rare bear. During the late fall and early winter evenings, hear the bugling of elk mating season.

ENDANGERED FAUNA & FLORA: Host to three threatened species of the Canada lynx, the Mexican Spotted Owl, and the North American wolverine.

MAIN ATTRACTIONS: The Continental Divide National Scenic Trail is a breathtaking 30 miles of high peaks, alpine tundra, and tree line scenery at elevations of 8,000 feet and above. Arrive early and spend the rest of the day fishing, camping, snowshoeing, and horseback riding at lower altitudes.

PRIMARY PURPOSE: To preserve the high-elevation ecosystems and diverse wilderness of the southern Rocky Mountains and to give recreational access to its natural features and cultural objects.

MONDAY (JULY)   **29**

TUESDAY (JULY)   **30**

WEDNESDAY (JULY)   **31**

THURSDAY   **1**

FRIDAY   **2**

SATURDAY   **3**

SUNDAY ◯   **4**

AUGUST 2024

MONDAY SUMMER BANK HOLIDAY (UK-SCT)   **5**

TUESDAY   **6**

WEDNESDAY   **7**

THURSDAY   **8**

FRIDAY   **9**

SATURDAY   **10**

SUNDAY   **11**

The land that the Rocky Mountain National Park sits
on was bought as part of the 1803 Louisiana Purchase.

AUGUST 2024

MONDAY) 12

TUESDAY 13

WEDNESDAY 14

THURSDAY 15

FRIDAY   **16**

SATURDAY   **17**

SUNDAY   **18**

The Alpine Visitor Center is the highest visitor center in the national park system, at an elevation of 11,796 feet.

AUGUST 2024

MONDAY ● 19

TUESDAY 20

WEDNESDAY 21

THURSDAY 22

FRIDAY   23

SATURDAY   24

SUNDAY   25

French author Jules Verne wrote about the park's highest point—Longs Peak—in his book FROM THE EARTH TO THE MOON (1865) before anyone in the world had successfully climbed it.

SEPTEMBER
Olympic National Park

Olympic National Park is a special place everyone seems to want to claim or recognize. Designated on *four* separate occasions: first as a national monument by Theodore Roosevelt in 1909, then as a National Park in 1938, then as an international biosphere reserve in 1976, and finally as a World Heritage Site in 1981. Located on the Olympic Peninsula in Washington State, it has three distinct ecosystems on top of a renowned sandy coastal strip stretching 60 miles end to end. Bring a camera to capture the views and some sturdy hiking boots to wade through the tidal pools, bushy overgrowth, and misty weather. Enter the glacial

zone, marked by the incredible Mount Olympus peak sitting 7,965 feet above sea level, and a wealth of other ridges and summits, like Mountain Deception if you want to try your hand at a truly memorable expedition. Explore more ancient glacial formations, such as the clear Lake Crescent, a great place for canoeing or picnicking with family. Visit the Queets Rainforest, where the ground is flat and more easily tread, for some solace and much-needed peace and quiet among the thick trees and temperate weather. Encompassing close to one million acres and thousands of years of history, Olympic National Park is a must-see destination.

SEPTEMBER 2024

NOTES	SUNDAY	MONDAY	TUESDAY
	1 ○	2	3
	FATHER'S DAY (AUS/NZ)	LABOR DAY (US) LABOUR DAY (CAN)	
	8	9	10
	GRANDPARENTS' DAY (US)		
	15	16 ●	17
	FIRST DAY OF NATIONAL HISPANIC HERITAGE MONTH		
	22	23 ◐	24
	FALL EQUINOX		
	29	30	

SEPTEMBER 2024

WEDNESDAY	THURSDAY	FRIDAY	SATURDAY
4	5	6	7
11	12	13	14
PATRIOT DAY (US) 18	19	20	21
25	26	27	28

OLYMPIC NATIONAL PARK

LOCATION: Western Washington

SIZE: 922,650 acres

BEST TIME TO VISIT: June through September

FAUNA & FLORA: An isolated peninsula comes with endemic species of fauna and flora you won't find elsewhere, including the Olympic marmot, Piper's bellflower, and Flett's violet.

ENDANGERED FAUNA & FLORA: The Short-tailed Albatross was brought to the brink of extinction by the plume trade in the 19th and early 20th centuries, and still remains endangered with a population of 7,300. Other threatened species include Northern Spotted Owls, Western Snowy Plovers, and Marbled Murrelets.

MAIN ATTRACTIONS: On the west side of the park, Kalaloch Beach is the ideal place to watch whales, sunsets, sea stacks, and tidepools in the summer. Enjoy boating, fishing, backpacking, and winter activities such as skiing, snowshoeing, and climbing.

PRIMARY PURPOSE: To preserve the primeval forest of Sitka spruce, western hemlock, and Douglas fir, and to provide suitable range and protection for indigenous wildlife.

AUGUST/SEPTEMBER

MONDAY (AUGUST) SUMMER BANK HOLIDAY (UK-ENG/NIR/WAL) ◖ **26**

TUESDAY (AUGUST) **27**

WEDNESDAY (AUGUST) **28**

THURSDAY (AUGUST) **29**

FRIDAY (AUGUST) **30**

SATURDAY (AUGUST) **31**

SUNDAY FATHER'S DAY (AUS/NZ) **1**

SEPTEMBER 2024

MONDAY LABOR DAY (US)/LABOUR DAY (CAN) ○ **2**

TUESDAY **3**

WEDNESDAY **4**

THURSDAY **5**

FRIDAY   **6**

SATURDAY   **7**

SUNDAY GRANDPARENTS' DAY (US)   **8**

At the stunning Lake Crescent, you can see about 60 feet deep. With its lack of nitrogen, the water is crystal clear to the naked eye.

SEPTEMBER 2024

MONDAY 9

TUESDAY 10

WEDNESDAY PATRIOT DAY (US) ▶ 11

THURSDAY 12

FRIDAY 13

SATURDAY 14

SUNDAY FIRST DAY OF NATIONAL HISPANIC HERITAGE MONTH 15

Through the Adopt-A-Fish project, you can catch, photograph, and radio tag your very own aquatic friend and provide the park with important information about their ecosystems.

SEPTEMBER 2024

MONDAY   **16**

TUESDAY ●   **17**

WEDNESDAY   **18**

THURSDAY   **19**

FRIDAY **20**

SATURDAY **21**

SUNDAY FALL EQUINOX **22**

The Hoh River marks the boundary between the southernmost part of the coastal segment and the Hoh Reservation, home to a tribe of 100 Indigenous people.

SEPTEMBER 2024

MONDAY   **23**

TUESDAY   **24**

WEDNESDAY   **25**

THURSDAY   **26**

FRIDAY

27

SATURDAY

28

SUNDAY

29

The Olympic Peninsula coast highway was named to pay homage to Greek explorer Juan de Fuca, who claimed to be the first to discover the Strait of Anián, near where the mountain range stands.

OCTOBER
Grand Canyon National Park

Grand Canyon National Park can best be described as a land of exceptional mythos, so bring plenty of water and plan to come early. It is the ideal vacation and tourist spot with nearly five million annual visitors. Prepare to be awed by the layers of colorful sedimentary rocks thousands of feet deep that date back to the earliest part of the Earth's history (the Precambrian period). From the Pueblo people worshipping the canyon as a holy site to acting as the destination for pilgrimages, to its current title as one of the natural wonders of the world, its mysticism is

unparalleled. Discover both the northern and southern rims by traversing the high points of the Grand Canyon by foot or mule, or stay close to the ground on a Desert View Drive with panoramic scenes of the Colorado River. Runners can enjoy a full 24 hours of scenery in the Grand Canyon Ultra Marathon, which spans 78 miles. Short on time? Just a 5-minute walk from the Visitor Center Plaza allows you to take photos at the Mather Point Overlook. Against the bold backdrop of red, pink, and orange rock layers, observe bats, bison, and toads.

OCTOBER 2024

NOTES	SUNDAY	MONDAY	TUESDAY
			1
	6	**7**	**8**
		LABOUR DAY (AUS-ACT/NSW/SA)	
	13	**14**	**15**
		INDIGENOUS PEOPLES' DAY (US) COLUMBUS DAY (US) THANKSGIVING DAY (CAN)	
	20	**21**	**22**
	27	**28**	**29**
		LABOUR DAY (NZ)	

OCTOBER 2024

WEDNESDAY	THURSDAY	FRIDAY	SATURDAY
○ 2	3	4	5
ROSH HASHANAH (BEGINS AT SUNDOWN)			
9 ☽	10	11	12
		YOM KIPPUR (BEGINS AT SUNDOWN)	
16 ●	17	18	19
SUKKOT (BEGINS AT SUNDOWN)			
23 ☾	24	25	26
	SIMCHAT TORAH (BEGINS AT SUNDOWN)		
30	31		
	HALLOWEEN		

GRAND CANYON NATIONAL PARK

LOCATION: Northwestern Arizona

SIZE: 1,217,262 acres

BEST TIME TO VISIT: May through November

FAUNA & FLORA: Containing five of the seven biological life zones, the park boasts more than 1,700 species of vascular plants and 90 species of mammals, with 22 of the latter being bats.

ENDANGERED FAUNA & FLORA: With incredible biodiversity comes a long list of endangered species, including California Condors, humpback chubs, razorback suckers, Willow Flycatchers, Kanab ambersnails, Ridgway's Rails, and Sentry milk-vetch.

MAIN ATTRACTIONS: The South Rim of the Grand Canyon is the most accessible, and therefore jam-packed with activities like the Verkamp and Market Plaza centers and the Historic District. Also walk the Trail of Time, bike, take a mule or raft trip, and so much more.

PRIMARY PURPOSE: To preserve the natural resources and ecological processes of the Grand Canyon and its scenic, aesthetic, and scientific aspects for public viewing and appreciation.

SEPTEMBER/OCTOBER

MONDAY (SEPTEMBER)   **30**

TUESDAY   **1**

WEDNESDAY ROSH HASHANAH (BEGINS AT SUNDOWN) ○   **2**

THURSDAY   **3**

FRIDAY   **4**

SATURDAY   **5**

SUNDAY   **6**

OCTOBER 2024

MONDAY LABOUR DAY (AUS-ACT/NSW/SA)

7

TUESDAY

8

WEDNESDAY

9

THURSDAY ◗

10

FRIDAY YOM KIPPUR (BEGINS AT SUNDOWN) **11**

SATURDAY **12**

SUNDAY **13**

Since 2010, Grand Canyon National Park has appeared on the U.S. quarter thanks to the America the Beautiful Quarters initiative commemorating historic sites from each state.

OCTOBER 2024

MONDAY INDIGENOUS PEOPLES' DAY (US)/COLUMBUS DAY (US)/ THANKSGIVING DAY (CAN) **14**

TUESDAY **15**

WEDNESDAY SUKKOT (BEGINS AT SUNDOWN) **16**

THURSDAY ● **17**

FRIDAY   **18**

SATURDAY   **19**

SUNDAY   **20**

The Grand Canyon is bigger than Rhode Island,
with 1,904 square miles compared to the state's
1,212 square miles.

OCTOBER 2024

MONDAY 21

TUESDAY 22

WEDNESDAY 23

THURSDAY SIMCHAT TORAH (BEGINS AT SUNDOWN) ◗ 24

FRIDAY

25

SATURDAY

26

SUNDAY

27

The most dangerous creatures in the park are not snakes or coyotes, but rock squirrels. Do not attempt to pet or take pictures with them.

NOVEMBER
Arches National Park

Established as a National Park in 1979, Arches National Park has been captivating visitors for decades. Home to more than 2,000 natural sandstone arches, the park is an eccentric beauty you won't find elsewhere—and it is all thanks to salt. Around 300 million years ago, the Paradox Basin was a sea that evaporated, leaving behind a rich bed of salt. That salt laid the foundation for the breathtaking arches, spires, and monoliths in the park. The park itself contains the highest density of natural arches worldwide. Make sure you have loads of storage left for photos of these natural phenomena, as these rocks are just for

looking at. After Dean Potter attempted his free climb of the Delicate Arch (52 feet high) in 2006, the park revised its regulations and eventually banned climbing altogether. Instead, go backpacking through the Hayduke Trail and encounter the flowing rivers, ridgelines, and drainages typical of the Colorado Plateau's high deserts. Toast s'mores and tell stories around the firepits at Devils Garden Campground in the heart of the park. For stargazers, plan nighttime visits and enjoy a certified International Dark Sky with uninhibited views of the majestic celestial bodies.

NOVEMBER 2024

NOTES	SUNDAY	MONDAY	TUESDAY
	3	4	5
			ELECTION DAY (US)
	10	11	12
		VETERANS DAY (US)	
	17	18	19
	24	25	26

NOVEMBER 2024

WEDNESDAY	THURSDAY	FRIDAY	SATURDAY
	○	1	2
		ALL SAINTS' DAY	
6	7	8 ◗	9
13	14 ●	15	16
20	21 ◖	22	23
27	28	29	30
	THANKSGIVING DAY (US)	NATIVE AMERICAN HERITAGE DAY (US)	

ARCHES NATIONAL PARK

LOCATION: Eastern Utah

SIZE: 76,519 acres

BEST TIME TO VISIT: March through October

FAUNA & FLORA: The harsh desert climate is home to animals and plants of the nocturnal and drought-resistant variety, respectively. Between dusk and dawn, find kangaroo rats, foxes, porcupines, and black-tailed jackrabbits roaming alongside the nine species of cactus, as well as cheatgrass and lichen.

ENDANGERED FAUNA & FLORA: Four of the six species of fish living in the Colorado River are endangered, including the bonytail and humpback chubs, razorback suckers, and Colorado pikeminnows.

MAIN ATTRACTIONS: One of the most iconic features is the 128-foot Balanced Rock noticeably tilted on its perch above Dewey Bridge mudstone. Also picnic, stargaze, backpack, bike, or go canyoneering.

PRIMARY PURPOSE: To protect extraordinary examples of geologic features and provide opportunities to explore these resources in their majestic natural settings.

MONDAY (OCTOBER) LABOUR DAY (NZ)   **28**

TUESDAY (OCTOBER)   **29**

WEDNESDAY (OCTOBER)   **30**

THURSDAY (OCTOBER) HALLOWEEN   **31**

FRIDAY ALL SAINTS' DAY ○   **1**

SATURDAY   **2**

SUNDAY   **3**

NOVEMBER 2024

MONDAY   **4**

TUESDAY ELECTION DAY (US)   **5**

WEDNESDAY   **6**

THURSDAY   **7**

FRIDAY   **8**

SATURDAY ◗   **9**

SUNDAY   **10**

The Fiery Furnace Trail is often described as a maze, with the lack of an established trail through twisting and turning canyons.

NOVEMBER 2024

MONDAY VETERANS DAY (US)   **11**

TUESDAY   **12**

WEDNESDAY   **13**

THURSDAY   **14**

FRIDAY ● **15**

SATURDAY **16**

SUNDAY **17**

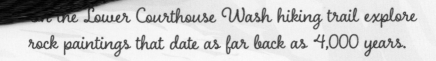

the Lower Courthouse Wash hiking trail explore rock paintings that date as far back as 4,000 years.

NOVEMBER 2024

MONDAY   **18**

TUESDAY   **19**

WEDNESDAY   **20**

THURSDAY   **21**

FRIDAY ◖

22

SATURDAY

23

SUNDAY

Wall Arch fell in 2008. People who were _____ ing at Devils Garden Campground that night _____ they thought they heard thunder but the skies _____ clear.

DECEMBER
Bryce Canyon National Park

Bryce Canyon National Park is named after Ebenezer Bryce, the Scottish immigrant sent to homestead the area in 1874. When other European settlers started to arrive, they termed it Bryce's Canyon. Bryce must have been overcome with gratitude, so much so he never got around to wondering why they chose to call it a "canyon" when there is no canyon to speak of in the park. Without getting too technical, they were referring to a collection of giant natural amphitheaters lining the Paunsaugunt Plateau. Tall hoodoos—or spire-shaped rock formations— form the famous horseshoe-shaped Bryce Amphitheater. Shaped by the drainage

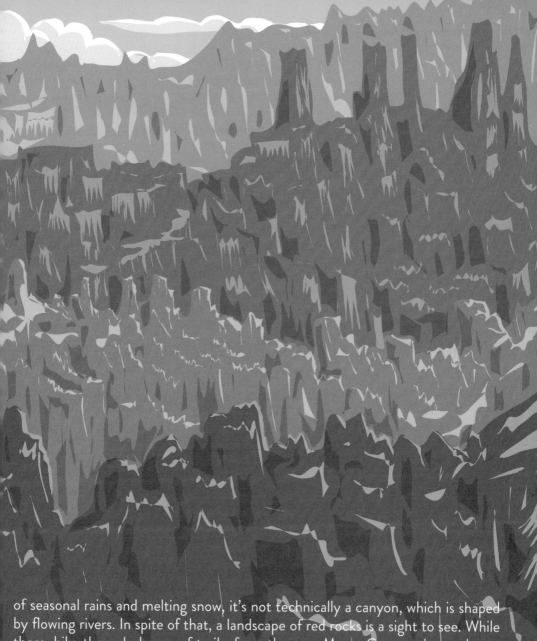

of seasonal rains and melting snow, it's not technically a canyon, which is shaped by flowing rivers. In spite of that, a landscape of red rocks is a sight to see. While there, hike through dozens of trails, from the easy Mossy Cave to the moderate Navajo Loop to the deceivingly strenuous Fairyland Trail. Come in time for the park's Geology Festival every mid-July and have fun on guided hikes, at hoodoo geology talks, and other activities best suited for the whole family. A more remote location near the Zion and Grand Canyons, Bryce Canyon National Park makes for an otherworldly experience.

DECEMBER 2024

NOTES	SUNDAY	MONDAY	TUESDAY
	○ 1	2	3
	WORLD AIDS DAY		INTERNATIONAL DAY OF PERSONS WITH DISABILITIES
	◐ 8	9	10
			HUMAN RIGHTS DAY
	● 15	16	17
	◐ 22	23	24
			CHRISTMAS EVE
	29	○ 30	31
			NEW YEAR'S EVE

DECEMBER 2024

WEDNESDAY	THURSDAY	FRIDAY	SATURDAY
4	5	6	7
11	12	13	14
18	19	20	21 WINTER SOLSTICE
25 CHRISTMAS DAY HANUKKAH (BEGINS AT SUNDOWN)	26 BOXING DAY (UK/CAN/AUS/NZ) FIRST DAY OF KWANZAA	27	28

BRYCE CANYON NATIONAL PARK

LOCATION: Southwestern Utah

SIZE: 35,835 acres

BEST TIME TO VISIT: June through December

FAUNA & FLORA: Home to 59 species of mammals, including the Uinta chipmunk and the pronghorn, which live at various elevations within the park. More than 175 species of birds have been documented. Find flowers like mountain death camas and showy rush pink across the landscape.

ENDANGERED FAUNA & FLORA: Currently, three endangered species live in the park: the Utah prairie dog, California Condor, and Southwestern Willow Flycatcher.

MAIN ATTRACTIONS: Bryce, Inspiration, Sunset, and Sunrise Points all provide unimpeded views of the Bryce Amphitheater, which spans 12 miles across. Visit for horseback riding, hiking, rock climbing, and camping.

PRIMARY PURPOSE: To protect and conserve the natural landscape of highly colored and eroded geological features for the benefit and enjoyment of the people.

MONDAY (NOVEMBER)   **25**

TUESDAY (NOVEMBER)   **26**

WEDNESDAY (NOVEMBER)   **27**

THURSDAY (NOVEMBER) THANKSGIVING DAY (US)   **28**

FRIDAY (NOVEMBER) NATIVE AMERICAN HERITAGE DAY (US)   **29**

SATURDAY (NOVEMBER)   **30**

SUNDAY WORLD AIDS DAY ⭕   **1**

DECEMBER 2024

MONDAY
2

TUESDAY INTERNATIONAL DAY OF PERSONS WITH DISABILITIES
3

WEDNESDAY
4

THURSDAY
5

FRIDAY   **6**

SATURDAY   **7**

SUNDAY ◗   **8**

Hitch a ride with the park's free shuttle service that will take you to all the must-see areas and trails.

DECEMBER 2024

MONDAY **9**

TUESDAY HUMAN RIGHTS DAY **10**

WEDNESDAY **11**

THURSDAY **12**

FRIDAY　　　　　　　　　　　　　　　　**13**

SATURDAY　　　　　　　　　　　　　　**14**

SUNDAY ●　　　　　　　　　　　　　　**15**

The park celebrated its 100-year anniversary on June 8, 2023, with a variety of virtual and in-person events occurring all through 2023. Find out what happened at #BRYCE100.

DECEMBER 2024

MONDAY 16

TUESDAY 17

WEDNESDAY 18

THURSDAY 19

FRIDAY

20

SATURDAY WINTER SOLSTICE

21

SUNDAY ◖

22

According to Paiute folklore, the hoodoos are said to have been people turned into stone by the trickster Coyote for their misdeeds.

DECEMBER 2024

MONDAY 23

TUESDAY CHRISTMAS EVE 24

WEDNESDAY CHRISTMAS DAY/HANUKKAH (BEGINS AT SUNDOWN) 25

THURSDAY BOXING DAY (UK/CAN/AUS/NZ)/FIRST DAY OF KWANZAA 26

FRIDAY 27

SATURDAY 28

SUNDAY 29

The Grand Staircase is believed to have the highest concentration of dinosaur fossils in the world.

JANUARY
Glacier National Park

Exploring the wintry wonderland of Glacier National Park is a limited time offer. Between 1966 and 2010, glaciers over 25 acres in size reduced from numbers of 150 to just 25, so place this one at the top of your list of National Parks to visit. Sitting on the Canada-U.S. border, Glacier National Park is part of the Crown of the Continent Biosphere Reserve, an exceptionally well-preserved piece of wilderness spanning 16,000 square miles and known for its pristine quality of carved valleys, lakes, and alpine meadows. Besides bison and woodland caribou, you can find all of Glacier's original native plant and animal species within the park, including Clark's

Nutcracker, the Canada Goose, and whitebark pine. Visit the brilliant turquoise and opaque Avalanche and Cracker Lakes, but skip taking the plunge. The 700 lakes within the park stay cold year-round. Instead, try your hand at kayaking or fly fishing with no permits necessary. A drive down Going-to-the-Sun Road will have you weaving among stunning views of Bird Woman Falls, Heaven's Peak, and Trail of the Cedars, the latter of which welcomes hikers. From the snowy alpine climate of the higher altitudes to the milder and wetter microclimates of the lower altitudes, Glacier National Park is rich in visual landscapes that are quickly disappearing.

JANUARY 2025

NOTES	SUNDAY	MONDAY	TUESDAY
		5 ◗ 6	7
	12 ● 13		14
	19	20 ◖ 21	
		CIVIL RIGHTS DAY (US) MARTIN LUTHER KING JR. DAY (US)	
	26	27	28
	AUSTRALIA DAY (AUS)	HOLOCAUST REMEMBRANCE DAY	

JANUARY 2025

WEDNESDAY	THURSDAY	FRIDAY	SATURDAY
1 NEW YEAR'S DAY	2 NEW YEAR HOLIDAY (UK-SCT)	3	4
8	9	10	11
15	16	17	18
22	23	24	25
○ 29 CHINESE NEW YEAR	30	31	

GLACIER NATIONAL PARK

LOCATION: Northwestern Montana

SIZE: 1,013,322 acres

BEST TIME TO VISIT: May through September

FAUNA & FLORA: With the vast majority of its original indigenous flora and fauna still intact, the park boasts more than 1,000 species of plants, 276 species of birds, and 64 types of mammals.

ENDANGERED FAUNA & FLORA: Aside from the melting glaciers themselves, currently endangered species include the little brown and northern myotis and whitebark pine. Wolves went extinct in 1936 due to their deliberate extermination by park rangers, but by the 1990s they managed to recolonize the area after a Canadian litter migrated to it.

MAIN ATTRACTIONS: At Logan Pass, the highest point of Going-to-the-Sun Road, witness a panoramic view of rainbow fields of wildflowers. Other activities include hiking, cycling, camping, and backpacking.

PRIMARY PURPOSE: To preserve the glacially shaped landscapes, wildlife, and heritage of the Crown of the Continent for the enjoyment and understanding of the public.

DECEMBER/JANUARY

MONDAY (DECEMBER) ○   **30**

TUESDAY (DECEMBER) NEW YEAR'S EVE   **31**

WEDNESDAY NEW YEAR'S DAY   **1**

THURSDAY NEW YEAR HOLIDAY (UK-SCT)   **2**

FRIDAY   **3**

SATURDAY   **4**

SUNDAY   **5**

JANUARY 2025

MONDAY)   **6**

TUESDAY   **7**

WEDNESDAY   **8**

THURSDAY   **9**

FRIDAY 10

SATURDAY 11

SUNDAY 12

Tune in to the park's own podcast, HEADWATERS, which talks about how Glacier National Park is connected to everything.

JANUARY 2025

MONDAY ● 13

TUESDAY 14

WEDNESDAY 15

THURSDAY 16

FRIDAY 17

SATURDAY 18

SUNDAY 19

Snowfall can occur year-round within Glacier National Park, even in the summer.

JANUARY 2025

MONDAY CIVIL RIGHTS DAY (US)/MARTIN LUTHER KING JR. DAY (US) **20**

TUESDAY ◗ **21**

WEDNESDAY **22**

THURSDAY **23**

FRIDAY 24

SATURDAY 25

SUNDAY AUSTRALIA DAY (AUS) 26

Glacier National Park borders the Canadian Waterton Lakes National Park in the north, and the two were jointly designated as the world's first international Peace Park in 1932.

FEBRUARY
Grand Teton National Park

Established in 1929 by President Calvin Coolidge, Grand Teton National Park is an outlaw among them all. While other National Parks have strict regulations against hunting or disturbing the natural wildlife, Grand Teton expressly encourages the opposite. As home of the National Elk Refuge—the largest elk herd in the world—the park contains thousands of elk open to hunters to help control the population. Also, unlike other parks that ban or severely limit snowshoeing, cross-country skiing, or snowmobiling, Grand Teton welcomes you to take to the slopes any way you see fit—even if veering outside the trails. With an incredible 40 miles of

snowcapped mountains in the Teton Range alone, there are plenty of options to choose from. On your visit to the park in the spring or summertime, bring a picnic or take a thrilling boat ride down the winding Snake River, more than 1,000 miles long, that empties into the Pacific. Thanks to the surrounding mountains, summers in Grand Teton are mild and therefore ideal for taxing activities such as hiking, biking, and mountaineering. With a mix of pristine lakes, remarkable wildlife, deep valleys, and alpine terrain to explore, Grand Teton is a scenic wonderland perfect for your next adventure.

FEBRUARY 2025

NOTES	SUNDAY	MONDAY	TUESDAY
	2	**3**	**4**
	GROUNDHOG DAY (US/CAN)		
	9	**10**	**11**
	16	**17**	**18**
		PRESIDENTS' DAY (US)	
	23	**24**	**25**

FEBRUARY 2025

WEDNESDAY	THURSDAY	FRIDAY	SATURDAY
			1 FIRST DAY OF BLACK HISTORY MONTH
◗ **5**	**6** WAITANGI DAY OBSERVED (NZ)	**7**	**8**
● **12**	**13**	**14** VALENTINE'S DAY	**15**
19	◗ **20**	**21**	**22**
26	○ **27**	**28** RAMADAN (BEGINS AT SUNDOWN)	

GRAND TETON NATIONAL PARK

LOCATION: Northwestern Wyoming

SIZE: 310,000 acres

BEST TIME TO VISIT: May through October

FAUNA & FLORA: In addition to the thousands of elk roaming around, wolverines, badgers, snowshoe hares, and river otters are commonly sighted. Past the 10,000-foot elevation mark, it is pure tundra devoid of any trees and instead filled with hundreds of grasses, wildflowers, moss, and lichen.

ENDANGERED FAUNA & FLORA: A number of threatened species include the Canada lynx, the western glacier stonefly, and the Yellow-billed Cuckoo. Grizzly bears nearly went extinct because of eradication programs, but today around 800 bears live in Grand Teton and the surrounding areas.

MAIN ATTRACTIONS: The pristine Jackson Lake stretches 15 miles in length and is one of the premier locations for camping in the park. In addition to its scenic views, enjoy mountaineering, fishing, or biking, all while being safe in bear country.

PRIMARY PURPOSE: To protect the Teton Range's major peaks and the area's indigenous plant- and wildlife, cultural and historic resources, and scenic values.

JANUARY/FEBRUARY

MONDAY (JANUARY) HOLOCAUST REMEMBRANCE DAY   **27**

TUESDAY (JANUARY)   **28**

WEDNESDAY (JANUARY) CHINESE NEW YEAR ○   **29**

THURSDAY (JANUARY)   **30**

FRIDAY (JANUARY)   **31**

SATURDAY FIRST DAY OF BLACK HISTORY MONTH   **1**

SUNDAY GROUNDHOG DAY (US/CAN)   **2**

FEBRUARY 2025

MONDAY **3**

TUESDAY **4**

WEDNESDAY ◗ **5**

THURSDAY WAITANGI DAY OBSERVED (NZ) **6**

FRIDAY 7

SATURDAY 8

SUNDAY 9

Off Teton Park Drive, stop at Mount Moran, Mountain View, Cascade Canyon, or Teton Glacier turnouts to get a great view of the Teton Range.

FEBRUARY 2025

MONDAY   **10**

TUESDAY   **11**

WEDNESDAY ●   **12**

THURSDAY   **13**

FRIDAY VALENTINE'S DAY

14

SATURDAY

15

SUNDAY

16

The name "Teton" comes from LES TROIS TÉTONS of early French-speaking mountain men sent to participate in the fur trade exploration in the early 19th century.

FEBRUARY 2025

MONDAY PRESIDENTS' DAY (US)   **17**

TUESDAY   **18**

WEDNESDAY   **19**

THURSDAY ☽   **20**

FRIDAY 21

SATURDAY 22

SUNDAY 23

Only 10 miles from Yellowstone, Grand Teton is actually considered part of the Greater Yellowstone Ecosystem.

MARCH
Sequoia National Park

Among the seemingly boundless landscape of tall, thick, and mountainous forests, we are extremely grateful for the unprofitability of sequoia trees. Before Sequoia National Park was established in 1890, European settlers attempted and failed to bring sequoia into the timber trade because of the trees' susceptibility to splintering. Had they been a tad more durable, the General Sherman Tree in Giant Forest— the largest tree on Earth by volume—might not exist. Today, the forests remain fairly undisturbed, with none being chopped down to create a central road through it, like many other National Parks. Instead of scenic drives and bus tours, explore

the wonders of Sequoia National Park on foot or horseback. In late spring, visit the 1,200-foot cascading Tokopah Falls when it is at its most powerful. By autumn, the churning, deep-blue falls will either be mere droplets or gone altogether. You won't have enough time in a single day to traverse all 400,000 acres of Sequoia National Park, but you can experience as much as possible with a venture to Moro Rock. Come face-to-face with the granite monolith as you take the stairway cut into it all the way to the top. From this vantage point, you can see the park in its entirety, inspiring a sense of wonder you will never forget.

MARCH 2025

NOTES	SUNDAY	MONDAY	TUESDAY
	2	**3**	**4**
	9	**10**	**11**
	16	LABOUR DAY (AUS-VIC) **17**	**18**
	23	ST. PATRICK'S DAY **24**	**25**
	MOTHERING SUNDAY (UK) EID AL-FITR (BEGINS AT SUNSET) **30**	**31**	

MARCH 2025

WEDNESDAY	THURSDAY	FRIDAY	SATURDAY
			1 FIRST DAY OF WOMEN'S HISTORY MONTH
5 ◗	**6**	**7**	**8**
12 ASH WEDNESDAY	**13** ●	**14**	**15**
19	**20** SPRING EQUINOX	**21** ◖ NOWRUZ	**22**
26	**27**	**28** ○	**29**

PURIM
(BEGINS AT SUNDOWN)

SEQUOIA NATIONAL PARK

LOCATION: South Central California

SIZE: 404,064 acres

BEST TIME TO VISIT: March through October

FAUNA & FLORA: The low altitudes tend to be dominated by blue oak woodlands and yucca plants, while the higher elevations have a mixture of ponderosa, sugar, and lodgepole pines. Commonly seen animals are bobcats, foxes, rattlesnakes, mule deer, and Pacific fishers.

ENDANGERED FAUNA & FLORA: The park is home to three endangered species of the mountain yellow-legged frog, Sierra Nevada yellow-legged frog, and bighorn sheep. However, there are plans to reintroduce bighorn sheep into the park through translocation efforts.

MAIN ATTRACTIONS: As the lowest east-west pass through the Great Western Divide, Kaweah Gap is an ideal spot where the whole family can confidently go hiking. Take a day hike to capture a quiet sunset, a mountain landscape, or a wondrous soundscape.

PRIMARY PURPOSE: To preserve and provide access to the natural and cultural resources of sequoia forests and the Sierra Nevada mountains.

FEBRUARY/MARCH

MONDAY (FEBRUARY)   **24**

TUESDAY (FEBRUARY)   **25**

WEDNESDAY (FEBRUARY)   **26**

THURSDAY (FEBRUARY) ○   **27**

FRIDAY (FEBRUARY) RAMADAN (BEGINS AT SUNDOWN)   **28**

SATURDAY FIRST DAY OF WOMEN'S HISTORY MONTH   **1**

SUNDAY   **2**

MARCH 2025

MONDAY **3**

TUESDAY **4**

WEDNESDAY ASH WEDNESDAY **5**

THURSDAY ◗ **6**

FRIDAY   **7**

SATURDAY   **8**

SUNDAY   **9**

Prior to the park's establishment, a calvary of men from
the U.S. Army's all-Black regiment, called the Buffalo
Soldiers, manned the area.

MARCH 2025

MONDAY LABOUR DAY (AUS-VIC) **10**

TUESDAY **11**

WEDNESDAY **12**

THURSDAY PURIM (BEGINS AT SUNDOWN) **13**

FRIDAY ● **14**

SATURDAY **15**

SUNDAY **16**

Sequoias need fire to survive as fire creates the most ideal conditions for regeneration success.

MARCH 2025

MONDAY ST. PATRICK'S DAY

17

TUESDAY

18

WEDNESDAY

19

THURSDAY SPRING EQUINOX

20

FRIDAY NOWRUZ

21

SATURDAY ◖

22

SUNDAY

23

Sequoia National Park is separated from Kings
Canyon National Park by the Great Western Divide;
the two were jointly designated as the Sequoia-Kings
Canyon Biosphere Reserve in 1976.

MARCH 2025

MONDAY 24

TUESDAY 25

WEDNESDAY 26

THURSDAY 27

FRIDAY   **28**

SATURDAY ○   **29**

SUNDAY MOTHERING SUNDAY (UK)/EID AL-FITR (BEGINS AT SUNSET) **30**

The biodiversity of Sequoia National Park cannot be understated, housing 11 species of woodpeckers alone.

APRIL
Acadia National Park

Between October and March, Acadia National Park is the first place in the country to see the sun rise. Established originally as a national monument in 1916 by Woodrow Wilson, the park is known as the Crown Jewel of the Atlantic Coast. The park's pioneering nature seemed to be contagious in the late 19th century, drawing iconic names to its glaciated coastal landscape such as the Carnegies, Astors, Vanderbilts, and Rockefellers. In fact, John D. Rockefeller Jr. financed and oversaw the construction of a historic carriage road system across Mount Desert Island, which today you can hike, bike, or ride horseback through. Drop by Somes

Sound, the 5-mile-long, icy fjard (a glacial embayment smaller than a true fjord) that nearly splits Mount Desert Island in half. Alongside Mount Desert Island, Acadia National Park also includes sections of Isle au Haut, the Schoodic Peninsula, and 16 smaller islands with sweeping views of the Atlantic Ocean, pine forests, and island lakes. Drive down Park Loop Road for an abridged version of the scenic highlights, including the Tarn, Thunder Hole, and Champlain Mountain. Alongside the Acadia Night Sky Festival every September, try ice fishing in the wintertime or swimming and tide pooling the crystal waters in the spring and summer.

APRIL 2025

NOTES	SUNDAY	MONDAY	TUESDAY
			1
			APRIL FOOLS' DAY
	6	**7**	**8**
	13	**14**	**15**
	PALM SUNDAY		
	◑ **20**	**21**	**22**
	EASTER ORTHODOX EASTER		EARTH DAY
	○ **27**	**28**	**29**

APRIL 2025

WEDNESDAY	THURSDAY	FRIDAY	SATURDAY
2	3 ☽	4	5
9	10	11 ●	12
			PASSOVER (BEGINS AT SUNDOWN)
16	17	18	19
		GOOD FRIDAY	
23	24	25	26
ADMINISTRATIVE PROFESSIONALS' DAY (US) YOM HASHOAH (BEGINS AT SUNDOWN)		ANZAC DAY (AUS/NZ)	
30			

ACADIA NATIONAL PARK

LOCATION: Northeast Maine

SIZE: 49,075 acres

BEST TIME TO VISIT: Year-round

FAUNA & FLORA: With more than 20% being wetland, there is an abundance of marsh plants and amphibian and marine life. The American eel, moose, bears, whales, and seabirds are commonly seen and caught.

ENDANGERED FAUNA & FLORA: Only two endangered species live in Acadia National Park: the Peregrine Falcon and the Bald Eagle.

MAIN ATTRACTIONS: Standing at 1,530 feet, Cadillac Mountain is the tallest mountain on the Atlantic Coast. Accessible by car, the summit offers an unobstructed view of the island landscape; you can also visit historic sights or go tide pooling, bird-watching, and stargazing.

PRIMARY PURPOSE: To preserve the ecological integrity, scenic beauty, and scientific values of the Acadia archipelago and Schoodic Peninsula.

MONDAY (MARCH) 31

TUESDAY APRIL FOOLS' DAY 1

WEDNESDAY 2

THURSDAY 3

FRIDAY ◗ 4

SATURDAY 5

SUNDAY 6

APRIL 2025

MONDAY 7

TUESDAY 8

WEDNESDAY 9

THURSDAY 10

FRIDAY   **11**

SATURDAY PASSOVER (BEGINS AT SUNDOWN) ●   **12**

SUNDAY PALM SUNDAY   **13**

More than 10,000 acres burned in a fire in October 1947. Luckily, with restoration efforts and regrowth throughout the decades, the damage has been fully healed.

APRIL 2025

MONDAY 14

TUESDAY 15

WEDNESDAY 16

THURSDAY 17

FRIDAY GOOD FRIDAY   **18**

SATURDAY   **19**

SUNDAY EASTER/ORTHODOX EASTER ◗   **20**

Cadillac Mountain was integral to the U.S. Army
during the Second World War as a base to detect
warcraft—its incredible height and coastal position
provide an ideal location to receive radar signals.

APRIL 2025

MONDAY **21**

TUESDAY EARTH DAY **22**

WEDNESDAY ADMINISTRATIVE PROFESSIONALS' DAY (US)/ YOM HASHOAH (BEGINS AT SUNDOWN) **23**

THURSDAY **24**

FRIDAY ANZAC DAY (AUS/NZ) **25**

SATURDAY **26**

SUNDAY ○ **27**

Acadia practices a Leave No Trace ethic, receiving recognition as a Gold Standard Site for its work in visitor education and resource monitoring.

MAY
Crater Lake National Park

Satisfy that childhood fascination and get up close and personal to a volcano. As the site of a now collapsed and inactive volcano, Crater Lake National Park is a dream come true for your inner child and children alike. The titular Crater Lake at the apex of the park is known for its brilliant blue color and perfectly clear water nearly 2,000 feet deep. As anomalous as a mountainous lake can get, Crater Lake was formed by the collapse of Mount Mazama about 7,700 years ago. With beautiful volcanic remnants, deep blue water, and cloud-skimming peaks, this is a majestic landscape. The truly legendary park—specifically among

the ancestors of the Klamath tribe—offers an abundance of places to visit, including Wizard Island, Sun Notch, and the Phantom Ship. During your visit, walk the sandy, barren lands of the Pumice Desert or ride horseback through the lush Pacific Crest Trail for an incredible adventure. With snow covering the park eight months out of the year, roads can remain closed through late spring. You don't want to miss out on this National Park, so plan in advance and visit in the summertime to get the best bang for your buck.

MAY 2025

NOTES	SUNDAY	MONDAY	TUESDAY
	◗ **4**	**5**	**6**
		LABOUR DAY (AUS-QLD) EARLY MAY BANK HOLIDAY (UK) CINCO DE MAYO	
	11 ●	**12**	**13**
	MOTHER'S DAY (US/CAN)		
	18	**19** ◖	**20**
		VICTORIA DAY (CAN)	
	25 ○	**26**	**27**
		SPRING BANK HOLIDAY (UK) MEMORIAL DAY (US)	

MAY 2025

WEDNESDAY	THURSDAY	FRIDAY	SATURDAY
	1	2	3
	FIRST DAY OF ASIAN AMERICAN AND PACIFIC ISLANDER HERITAGE MONTH		
7	8	9	10
14	15	16	17
21	22	23	24
28	29	30	31

CRATER LAKE NATIONAL PARK

LOCATION: Southern Oregon

SIZE: 183,224 acres

BEST TIME TO VISIT: June through October

FAUNA & FLORA: Spot a black bear in early autumn and late spring. Golden-mantled ground squirrels, Canada Jays, and bees are other common fauna, as well as more than 700 species of native plants.

ENDANGERED FAUNA & FLORA: Both the bull trout and the Mazama newt are endangered species, the latter of which only exists in Crater Lake National Park.

MAIN ATTRACTIONS: The Rim Drive is one of the most popular scenic routes, as it follows the caldera rim and leads through beautiful vistas, forests, and meadows. This park is perfect for artists, photographers, and sightseers alike.

PRIMARY PURPOSE: To preserve and enhance Crater Lake's water purity, landscapes, volcanic features, and heritage for human inspiration and learning.

MONDAY (APRIL)   **28**

TUESDAY (APRIL)   **29**

WEDNESDAY (APRIL)   **30**

THURSDAY   FIRST DAY OF ASIAN AMERICAN AND PACIFIC ISLANDER HERITAGE MONTH   **1**

FRIDAY   **2**

SATURDAY   **3**

SUNDAY ◗   **4**

MAY 2025

MONDAY LABOUR DAY (AUS-QLD)/EARLY MAY BANK HOLIDAY (UK)/CINCO DE MAYO **5**

TUESDAY **6**

WEDNESDAY **7**

THURSDAY **8**

FRIDAY   **9**

SATURDAY   **10**

SUNDAY MOTHER'S DAY (US/CAN)   **11**

Established in 1902 by President Theodore Roosevelt,
Crater Lake is the 5th oldest National Park in
the U.S.

MAY 2025

MONDAY ●   **12**

TUESDAY   **13**

WEDNESDAY   **14**

THURSDAY   **15**

FRIDAY 16

SATURDAY 17

SUNDAY 18

Be aware of the "camp robbers" in the form of the corvid bird family, as they will take any opportunity to steal your unattended food.

MAY 2025

MONDAY VICTORIA DAY (CAN)

19

TUESDAY ☾

20

WEDNESDAY

21

THURSDAY

22

FRIDAY 23

SATURDAY 24

SUNDAY 25

Trolley tours run through July to mid-September for a luxury experience of the historic 33-mile Rim Drive.

JUNE
Yosemite National Park

Yosemite National Park is home to giant ancient sequoias, pines, and cedars; wild bears and deer; and breathtaking meadows. The designated wilderness composes 95 percent of the park today, although the park is best known for its waterfalls. Explore the thousands of picturesque lakes, ponds, streams, and forests deep in the Sierra Nevada. After you have witnessed it, there will be no wonder why Abraham Lincoln declared Yosemite as a preserved land in 1864. Yosemite paved the way for the National Park system altogether and continues to do so with the reverence and intrigue that surrounds it. It offers a diverse

range of climbing routes and year-round accessibility, including El Capitan. Take a hike to Wawona and the Mariposa Grove of Giant Sequoias, Hetch Hetchy, or Tuolumne Meadows. Visit the charming Crane Flat Campground northwest of the famous Yosemite Valley. Meadows of colorful wildflowers stun in the warmer months before the winter turns it into perfect skiing and snowshoeing trails. Do not miss out on the waterfalls! In the park, 25 breathtaking streams fall from as high as 2,400 feet. Bring your camera and some rain boots and experience all that Yosemite National Park has to offer.

JUNE 2025

NOTES	SUNDAY	MONDAY	TUESDAY
	1 FIRST DAY OF PRIDE MONTH	**2**	**3**
	8	**9**	**10**
	15 FATHER'S DAY (US/CAN/UK)	**16**	**17**
	22	**23**	**24**
	29	**30**	

JUNE 2025

WEDNESDAY	THURSDAY	FRIDAY	SATURDAY
4	5	6	7
● 11	12	13	14 FLAG DAY (US)
◐ 18	19	20	21
○ 25	26 JUNETEENTH (US)	27 SUMMER SOLSTICE	28

YOSEMITE NATIONAL PARK

LOCATION: Central California

SIZE: 759,620 acres

BEST TIME TO VISIT: November through April

FAUNA & FLORA: Black bears are notorious residents as they frequently break into parked cars to steal food. Also, find more than 165 species of migrating, wintering, and breeding birds, as well as 20% of California's total plant species.

ENDANGERED FAUNA & FLORA: The Sierra Nevada bighorn sheep, California wolverine, and Pacific fisher are the only endangered species in the park, but 14 other species are currently threatened.

MAIN ATTRACTIONS: With tons of winter activities, the holidays are the perfect time to visit. Curry Village Rink welcomes ice skaters of all ages, Yosemite Hospitality operates a snow tubing hill for sledding, and Badger Pass Ski Area contains a large network of marked winter routes for cross-country skiing.

PRIMARY PURPOSE: To preserve the towering waterfalls, steep cliffs, scenic rivers, and natural wilderness of the Sierra Nevada, and to celebrate its cultural and historic traditions for scientific exploration, recreation, and education for years to come.

MAY/JUNE

MONDAY (MAY) SPRING BANK HOLIDAY (UK)/MEMORIAL DAY (US) ○   **26**

TUESDAY (MAY)   **27**

WEDNESDAY (MAY)   **28**

THURSDAY (MAY)   **29**

FRIDAY (MAY)   **30**

SATURDAY (MAY)   **31**

SUNDAY FIRST DAY OF PRIDE MONTH   **1**

JUNE 2025

MONDAY ◗ 2

TUESDAY 3

WEDNESDAY 4

THURSDAY 5

FRIDAY 6

SATURDAY 7

SUNDAY 8

The Bracebridge Dinner—a holiday celebration inspired by Washington Irving's "Bracebridge Hall"—is held every year at the historic Ahwahnee Hotel.

JUNE 2025

MONDAY 9

TUESDAY 10

WEDNESDAY ● 11

THURSDAY 12

FRIDAY 13

SATURDAY FLAG DAY (US) 14

SUNDAY FATHER'S DAY (US/CAN/UK) 15

At sunset, the rock formations of El Capitan and Half Dome actually glow when light is reflected onto them, a phenomenon you can only witness in mid-February.

MONDAY **16**

TUESDAY **17**

WEDNESDAY ◖ **18**

THURSDAY JUNETEENTH (US) **19**

FRIDAY SUMMER SOLSTICE   **20**

SATURDAY   **21**

SUNDAY   **22**

In addition to rainbows, moonbows are a sight to see when the night skies are clear.

JUNE 2025

MONDAY **23**

TUESDAY **24**

WEDNESDAY ○ **25**

THURSDAY **26**

FRIDAY 27

SATURDAY 28

SUNDAY 29

Yosemite National Park was designated a World Heritage Site by UNESCO in 1984.

JULY
Cuyahoga Valley National Park

Few may know that the titular Cuyahoga River actually flows in reverse. Before the retreat of glaciers during the last ice age 10,000 to 12,000 years ago, the river originally flowed southward before redirecting north toward Lake Erie. The new current also forces the river to wrap around the remaining glacial debris in the area, causing it to take on the whimsical, winding shape it still holds today. With the river as the most prominent feature of Cuyahoga Valley National Park, a visit will be woefully incomplete without a riverside picnic or taking a paddle in a canoe down the river itself. Established in 2000 by Congress, Cuyahoga is one

of the youngest National Parks on the roster and therefore contains a unique mixture of natural and man-made features. There are narrow ravines, wetlands, and more than 100 falls, including the daunting 65-foot-tall Brandywine. Take a break from the monotony with a tour of the 19th-century Hale Farm and Village near Bath, Ohio. Or embrace nature's best while hunting for treasure with one of the plentiful guides offered by the park. With proximity to two large urban areas, there are also plenty of establishments to take refuge from Cuyahoga's hot and humid climate.

JULY 2025

NOTES	SUNDAY	MONDAY	TUESDAY
			1 CANADA DAY (CAN)
	6	**7**	**8**
	13	**14**	**15**
	20	**21**	**22**
	27	**28**	**29**

JULY 2025

WEDNESDAY	THURSDAY	FRIDAY	SATURDAY
☽	2	3	4 INDEPENDENCE DAY (US)	5
9 ●	10	11	12
16 ☾	17	18	19
23 ○	24	25	26
30	31		

CUYAHOGA VALLEY NATIONAL PARK

LOCATION: Northern Ohio

SIZE: 33,000 acres

BEST TIME TO VISIT: March through September

FAUNA & FLORA: Some of the most beautiful plants are the plethora of wildflowers like violets, toothwort, and rue anemone dotting the forest and wetland landscape. Common animal sightings include falcons, white-tailed deer, Great Blue Herons, and opossums.

ENDANGERED FAUNA & FLORA: The Indiana bat has been on the endangered species list since 1967. Between 2002 and 2022, the species could only be observed in Cuyahoga Valley National Park. However, it has not been found in the park since 2022.

MAIN ATTRACTIONS: From now until 2025, a traveling exhibit on pollination will move through different areas of the park. Also go hiking, golfing, kayaking, snowshoeing, or cross-country skiing, or take a historic train ride.

PRIMARY PURPOSE: To preserve the flora and fauna endemic to Cuyahoga Valley, and to provide recreation and solitude for Ohio's residents and visitors.

MONDAY (JUNE)   **30**

TUESDAY CANADA DAY (CAN)   **1**

WEDNESDAY ◗   **2**

THURSDAY   **3**

FRIDAY INDEPENDENCE DAY (US)   **4**

SATURDAY   **5**

SUNDAY   **6**

JULY 2025

MONDAY 7

TUESDAY 8

WEDNESDAY 9

THURSDAY ● 10

FRIDAY 11

SATURDAY 12

SUNDAY 13

The Buckeye Trail is a challenging trail with a great payoff—the beautiful Blue Hen Falls.

JULY 2025

MONDAY **14**

TUESDAY **15**

WEDNESDAY **16**

THURSDAY ☾ **17**

FRIDAY   **18**

SATURDAY   **19**

SUNDAY   **20**

*No one knows how the name "Cuyahoga" came to be—
it could be derived from the Mohawk word meaning
"crooked river" or the Seneca word for "jawbone."*

JULY 2025

MONDAY 21

TUESDAY 22

WEDNESDAY 23

THURSDAY ◯ 24

FRIDAY **25**

SATURDAY **26**

SUNDAY **27**

Sustainable farming ventures help preserve the valley's agricultural heritage, like the remains of the Ohio and Erie Canals.

AUGUST
Yellowstone National Park

As iconic as Yellowstone is, established in 1872 as the U.S.'s first ever National Park, many are hesitant to visit because of paranoia around its most notable feature: the Yellowstone Caldera. This sleeping beauty has significantly changed the country's landscape with its eruptions, its most violent occurring 2.1 million years ago, creating both the Huckleberry Ridge Tuff and the Island Park Caldera. But fear not—scientists are convinced that another super-eruption is *not* imminent or even possible based on the caldera's magma levels, so do not let it keep you away. As part of the South Central Rockies, the vast majority of

Yellowstone is comprised of deep, lush forests ripe for camping and spotting wolves, bears, and bison from a safe distance. Be swept away by the Grand Prismatic Spring, named for the rainbow of rich and striking colors that surround the immaculate water on all sides. The extensive forests of Yellowstone are rivaled only by its geysers, with half of the entire world's geysers in the park. Boasting an eruption every two hours, Old Faithful Geyser has an average eruption height of 145 feet. What a dazzlingly unforgettable moment to witness.

AUGUST 2025

NOTES	SUNDAY	MONDAY	TUESDAY
	3	**4**	**5**
		SUMMER BANK HOLIDAY (UK-SCT)	
	10	**11**	**12**
	17	**18**	**19**
	24	**25**	**26**
	☽ **31**		
		SUMMER BANK HOLIDAY (UK-ENG/NIR/WAL)	

AUGUST 2025

WEDNESDAY	THURSDAY	FRIDAY	SATURDAY
		☽ 1	2
6	7	8 ●	9
13	14	15 ☾	16
20	21	22 ○	23
27	28	29	30

YELLOWSTONE NATIONAL PARK

LOCATION: Northwest Wyoming

SIZE: 2,219,791 acres

BEST TIME TO VISIT: May through October

FAUNA & FLORA: More than 69,000 species of trees and vascular plants are native to the park, including the endemic Yellowstone sand verbena. The park is also home to a healthy roster of wildlife, with the largest public herd of bison in all 50 states.

ENDANGERED FAUNA & FLORA: The Canada lynx, gray wolf, grizzly bear, and black-footed ferret are all endangered species within Yellowstone.

MAIN ATTRACTIONS: Yellowstone Lake is the single-largest high-elevation lake in the country, sitting more than 7,000 feet above sea level over the Yellowstone Caldera. Explore in the summer with hiking, camping, and horseback riding, or in the winter with snowmobiling, skiing, and snowshoeing.

PRIMARY PURPOSE: To preserve and protect the two million acres of wilderness, mountains, geysers, and vibrant geothermal features for generations to come.

MONDAY (JULY) 28

TUESDAY (JULY) 29

WEDNESDAY (JULY) 30

THURSDAY (JULY) 31

FRIDAY) 1

SATURDAY 2

SUNDAY 3

AUGUST 2025

MONDAY SUMMER BANK HOLIDAY (UK-SCT)   4

TUESDAY   5

WEDNESDAY   6

THURSDAY   7

FRIDAY   **8**

SATURDAY ●   **9**

SUNDAY   **10**

Walk on the boardwalks and maintained trails to witness hot springs, mud pots, and geysers up close and personal.

AUGUST 2025

MONDAY 11

TUESDAY 12

WEDNESDAY 13

THURSDAY 14

FRIDAY 15

SATURDAY 16

SUNDAY 17

Geysers make for a natural laundry machine—European settlers noted that Old Faithful thoroughly washed cotton and linen with no issues, although it did shred wool.

AUGUST 2025

MONDAY 18

TUESDAY 19

WEDNESDAY 20

THURSDAY 21

FRIDAY

22

SATURDAY ○

23

SUNDAY

24

The most powerful earthquake to strike the park was the 1959 Hebgen Lake earthquake, opening new geysers and turning the water in existing hot springs opaque.

AUGUST 2025

MONDAY SUMMER BANK HOLIDAY (UK-ENG/NIR/WAL) **25**

TUESDAY **26**

WEDNESDAY **27**

THURSDAY **28**

FRIDAY   **29**

SATURDAY   **30**

SUNDAY   **31**

No mountaineering is allowed at Yellowstone because
the mountains within the park are largely comprised of
unstable volcanic rock.

SEPTEMBER
Great Smoky Mountains National Park

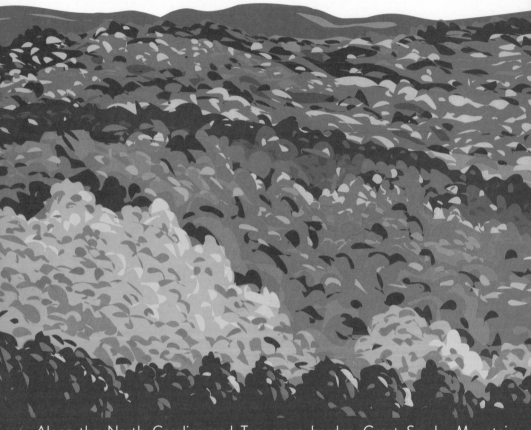

Along the North Carolina and Tennessee border, Great Smoky Mountains National Park holds the title of the most visited National Park in the entire country. The titular mountains are part of the larger Appalachian chain, which contains some of the highest mountains on the East Coast. Behold the highest point in the park, the Clingmans Dome, at an astonishing 6,643 feet. Or visit Mount Le Conte, the highest point that provides lodging for travelers seeking a longer stay. Around 95 percent of the park is forested, but between patches of deciduous and coniferous trees you can stumble across highlights like Roaring

Fork, the winding, volatile stream known for its roaring waters. Amplified by its proximity to surrounding mountain ridges, the area played home to a sizable Appalachian community, as seen by the preserved homes and buildings. Explore the immensely popular Cades Cove, where the erosion of sandstone unveils a beautiful, thick layer of limestone hidden underneath. Or traverse Deep Creek Loop, where alongside more streams, the Juney Whank Falls and Indian Creek Falls take center stage. With a humid subtropical climate, Great Smoky Mountains National Park is full of amazing opportunities in summer.

SEPTEMBER 2025

NOTES	SUNDAY	MONDAY	TUESDAY
		1	**2**
		LABOR DAY (US) LABOUR DAY (CAN)	
	● **7**	**8**	**9**
	GRANDPARENTS' DAY (US) FATHER'S DAY (AUS/NZ)		
	◑ **14**	**15**	**16**
		FIRST DAY OF NATIONAL HISPANIC HERITAGE MONTH	
	○ **21**	**22**	**23**
		FALL EQUINOX ROSH HASHANAH (BEGINS AT SUNDOWN)	
	28 ◗	**29**	**30**

SEPTEMBER 2025

WEDNESDAY	THURSDAY	FRIDAY	SATURDAY
3	4	5	6
10	11	12	13
	PATRIOT DAY (US)		
17	18	19	20
24	25	26	27

GREAT SMOKY MOUNTAINS NATIONAL PARK

LOCATION: Border of Tennessee and North Carolina

SIZE: 522,419 acres

BEST TIME TO VISIT: May through September

FAUNA & FLORA: Elk were successfully reintroduced in 2001, joining raccoons, bobcats, squirrels, and coyotes. There are 1,400 flowering plant species and 4,000 non-flowering plant species all around the park.

ENDANGERED FAUNA & FLORA: The northern flying squirrel, Red-cockaded Woodpecker, Indiana bat, spruce-fir moss spider, smoky madtom, spreading avens, and rock gnome lichen are endangered at the park. Efforts to reintroduce red wolves from 1991 to 1998 unfortunately failed.

MAIN ATTRACTIONS: Newfound Gap is the lowest drivable pass in the park. A stop along the pass allows you to stand in both Tennessee and North Carolina at the same time. Otherwise, go biking, fishing, hiking, camping, and horseback riding. In the wintertime, cross-country skiing is popular in the surrounding area.

PRIMARY PURPOSE: To preserve the historic structures, pristine landscapes, and artifacts of the Great Smoky Mountains, and to tell the stories of those who once called the mountains home.

SEPTEMBER

MONDAY LABOR DAY (US)/LABOUR DAY (CAN)

1

TUESDAY

2

WEDNESDAY

3

THURSDAY

4

FRIDAY

5

SATURDAY

6

SUNDAY GRANDPARENTS' DAY (US)/FATHER'S DAY (AUS/NZ) ●

7

SEPTEMBER 2025

MONDAY — 8

TUESDAY — 9

WEDNESDAY — 10

THURSDAY PATRIOT DAY (US) — 11

FRIDAY   **12**

SATURDAY   **13**

SUNDAY ◖   **14**

The word "Cataloochee," the namesake of Cataloochee
Valley, means "fringe standing erect" in Cherokee,
likely referring to the trees on the ridges surrounding
the valley.

SEPTEMBER 2025

MONDAY FIRST DAY OF NATIONAL HISPANIC HERITAGE MONTH   **15**

TUESDAY   **16**

WEDNESDAY   **17**

THURSDAY   **18**

FRIDAY   **19**

SATURDAY   **20**

SUNDAY ○   **21**

Visit the observation tower at the top of Clingmans
Dome to get a scenic view of the mist-covered mountains.

SEPTEMBER 2025

MONDAY FALL EQUINOX/ROSH HASHANAH (BEGINS AT SUNDOWN) **22**

TUESDAY **23**

WEDNESDAY **24**

THURSDAY **25**

FRIDAY 26

SATURDAY 27

SUNDAY 28

Great Smoky Mountains National Park has motor vehicle-free days every Wednesday between May and September in Cades Cove, so opt for your bike for a peaceful ride!

OCTOBER
Hot Springs National Park

An urban park, Hot Springs National Park has quite possibly one of the most fascinating human histories around. Originally traversed by Native Americans, the land was first bought during the Louisiana Purchase of 1803 and established as a federal reservation in 1832. At the onset, people were free to mine, build, and transform the area for decades, resulting in Downtown Hot Springs. The town stood until 1878, when a massive fire burned down a large number of the structures. After, the government administered the site, transforming the rough frontier town into an elegant spa with the titular hot springs as its showstopping feature. An icon

of the American spa and a National Historic Landmark District, the original eight bathhouses standing in Bathhouse Row are open for tours. Admire the beautiful architecture and history as you stroll along the Grand Promenade. In the case of Buckstaff and Quapaw Boathouses, take advantage of their spa services and take a soak in them yourself. Gather your family and pets for an educational tour and experience the area still known as Downtown Hot Springs. The natural curiosities of the ancient thermal springs are unmatched with mountain views, forested hikes, and abundant creeks—all in the middle of town.

OCTOBER 2025

NOTES	SUNDAY	MONDAY	TUESDAY
	5 ●	**6**	**7**
		LABOUR DAY (AUS-ACT/NSW/SA) SUKKOT (BEGINS AT SUNDOWN)	
	12 ◖	**13**	**14**
		INDIGENOUS PEOPLES' DAY (US) COLUMBUS DAY (US) THANKSGIVING DAY (CAN)	SIMCHAT TORAH (BEGINS AT SUNDOWN)
	19	**20** ○	**21**
	26	**27**	**28**
		LABOUR DAY (NZ)	

OCTOBER 2025

WEDNESDAY	THURSDAY	FRIDAY	SATURDAY
1	2	3	4
YOM KIPPUR (BEGINS AT SUNSET)			
8	9	10	11
15	16	17	18
22	23	24	25
29	30	31	
		HALLOWEEN	

HOT SPRINGS NATIONAL PARK

LOCATION: Central Arkansas

SIZE: 5,550 acres

BEST TIME TO VISIT: February through September

FAUNA & FLORA: While the forests are dominated by hickory, pine, and oak vegetation, the roster of animals is much more diverse, with 50 species of mammals, 100 species of birds, and 70 species of reptiles, including salamanders and armadillos.

ENDANGERED FAUNA & FLORA: Uniquely, Hot Springs National Park contains zero endangered or even threatened species.

MAIN ATTRACTIONS: Standing tall at 1,256 feet above sea level, the observation deck on Hot Springs Mountain Tower overlooks the entire park and is the best spot to admire all of the beautiful scenery within it. In addition to camping, birding, and biking, you can eat at a variety of diners and roam the shops.

PRIMARY PURPOSE: To preserve and protect the natural lithology, geologic structure, and thermal hot springs of Hot Springs Reservation.

SEPTEMBER/OCTOBER

MONDAY (SEPTEMBER) ◗ **29**

TUESDAY (SEPTEMBER) **30**

WEDNESDAY YOM KIPPUR (BEGINS AT SUNSET) **1**

THURSDAY **2**

FRIDAY **3**

SATURDAY **4**

SUNDAY **5**

OCTOBER 2025

MONDAY LABOUR DAY (AUS-ACT/NSW/SA)/SUKKOT (BEGINS AT SUNDOWN) ● **6**

TUESDAY **7**

WEDNESDAY **8**

THURSDAY **9**

FRIDAY

10

SATURDAY

11

SUNDAY

12

Bring your dog to be officially sworn in as a B.A.R.K. Ranger by completing activities to earn a certificate.

OCTOBER 2025

MONDAY INDIGENOUS PEOPLES' DAY (US)/COLUMBUS DAY (US)/
THANKSGIVING DAY (CAN)   **13**

TUESDAY SIMCHAT TORAH (BEGINS AT SUNDOWN)   **14**

WEDNESDAY   **15**

THURSDAY   **16**

FRIDAY 17

SATURDAY 18

SUNDAY 19

The hot springs are fed by rainwater on the mountains north of the park that migrates underneath the surface—to a minimum depth of 4,500 feet—emerging once the temperature reaches boiling point.

OCTOBER 2025

MONDAY 20

TUESDAY ○ 21

WEDNESDAY 22

THURSDAY 23

FRIDAY 24

SATURDAY 25

SUNDAY 26

Spa visits began as far back as 8,000 years ago because of the water's healing effects, which benefit skin, blood, and nervous system diseases in addition to rheumatism.

NOVEMBER
Zion National Park

Back in the Jurassic Age, the area encompassing Zion National Park was as hugely barren, arid, and magnificent as the Sahara Desert is today. Established in 1919, Zion National Park bridges the Colorado Plateau, Great Basin, and Mojave Desert, and as a result, possesses a wide variety of awe-inspiring formations. The Navajo Sandstone constitutes some of the park's most iconic features across the Colorado Plateau and fully blankets the region. Discover the Checkerboard Mesa, an iconic rock formation and a remnant of ancient dunes named for the visible lines embedded deep in the Navajo Sandstone. They are easily spotted along

Highway 9, so load your car with friends and snacks and head out for a leisurely scenic drive. Adventurers can take the 16-mile hike of Virgin River Narrows, estimated to be 10 to 14 hours long. Hiking through the river, under the shadow of soaring walls, sandstone grottos, natural springs, and hanging gardens is an unforgettable experience. About 80 percent of the route is spent wading, walking, and swimming sections of the river, so be sure to plan ahead with water shoes and life vests. Wherever you are in the park, bring extra water to face the blazing heat of the desert as you explore all that Zion has to offer.

NOVEMBER 2025

NOTES	SUNDAY	MONDAY	TUESDAY
	2	3	4
			ELECTION DAY (US)
	9	10	11
			VETERANS DAY (US)
	16	17	18
	23	24	25
	30		

NOVEMBER 2025

WEDNESDAY	THURSDAY	FRIDAY	SATURDAY
			1
			ALL SAINTS' DAY
● 5	6	7	8
◗ 12	13	14	15
19 ○	20	21	22
26	27 ◗	28	29
	THANKSGIVING DAY (US)	NATIVE AMERICAN HERITAGE DAY (US)	

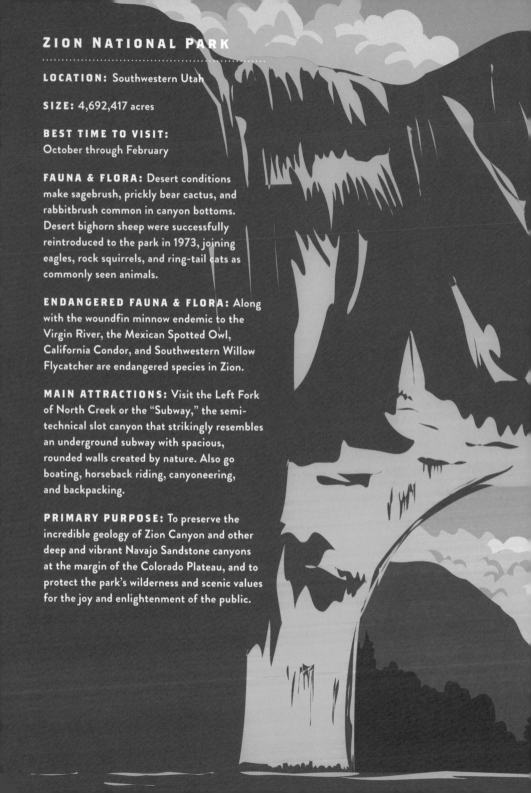

ZION NATIONAL PARK

LOCATION: Southwestern Utah

SIZE: 4,692,417 acres

BEST TIME TO VISIT:
October through February

FAUNA & FLORA: Desert conditions
make sagebrush, prickly bear cactus, and
rabbitbrush common in canyon bottoms.
Desert bighorn sheep were successfully
reintroduced to the park in 1973, joining
eagles, rock squirrels, and ring-tail cats as
commonly seen animals.

ENDANGERED FAUNA & FLORA: Along
with the woundfin minnow endemic to the
Virgin River, the Mexican Spotted Owl,
California Condor, and Southwestern Willow
Flycatcher are endangered species in Zion.

MAIN ATTRACTIONS: Visit the Left Fork
of North Creek or the "Subway," the semi-
technical slot canyon that strikingly resembles
an underground subway with spacious,
rounded walls created by nature. Also go
boating, horseback riding, canyoneering,
and backpacking.

PRIMARY PURPOSE: To preserve the
incredible geology of Zion Canyon and other
deep and vibrant Navajo Sandstone canyons
at the margin of the Colorado Plateau, and to
protect the park's wilderness and scenic values
for the joy and enlightenment of the public.

OCTOBER/NOVEMBER

MONDAY (OCTOBER) LABOUR DAY (NZ)

27

TUESDAY (OCTOBER)

28

WEDNESDAY (OCTOBER) ◗

29

THURSDAY (OCTOBER)

30

FRIDAY (OCTOBER) HALLOWEEN

31

SATURDAY ALL SAINTS' DAY

1

SUNDAY

2

NOVEMBER 2025

MONDAY 3

TUESDAY ELECTION DAY (US) 4

WEDNESDAY ● 5

THURSDAY 6

FRIDAY   **7**

SATURDAY   **8**

SUNDAY   **9**

Anticipate heavy rains in late spring. When the park
was inundated in 1995, the water caused a landslide
that blocked the exit roads in Zion Canyon and briefly
trapped 450 guests and employees.

NOVEMBER 2025

MONDAY 10

TUESDAY VETERANS DAY (US) 11

WEDNESDAY ☾ 12

THURSDAY 13

FRIDAY 14

SATURDAY 15

SUNDAY 16

Horse Ranch Mountain is the highest point in Zion National Park, with a summit of 8,726 feet above sea level.

NOVEMBER 2025

MONDAY **17**

TUESDAY **18**

WEDNESDAY **19**

THURSDAY ○ **20**

FRIDAY   **21**

SATURDAY   **22**

SUNDAY   **23**

The Zion region was originally named Mukuntuweap
by President Howard Taft in his 1909 proclamation to
protect the area, but was changed to Zion in 1918 to avoid
mispronunciation.

NOVEMBER 2025

MONDAY   **24**

TUESDAY   **25**

WEDNESDAY   **26**

THURSDAY   THANKSGIVING DAY (US)   **27**

FRIDAY NATIVE AMERICAN HERITAGE DAY (US) ☽ **28**

SATURDAY **29**

SUNDAY **30**

The park's canyon formations are a part of the Grand Staircase rock super-sequence that stretches all the way south to Bryce Canyon National Park in Utah.

DECEMBER
Shenandoah National Park

The road to establishing Shenandoah National Park was long and arduous. It took an entire decade of the Virginia state government employing its state funds, power of eminent domain, and private donations before Shenandoah National Park was established on December 26, 1935. Unhelpful to the acquisition process was the sheer enormity of the region, encompassing parts of eight different counties in Virginia through its dominant feature—the Blue Ridge Mountain range. The mountain range was formed around 400 million years ago, yet the bedrock of the park is even older, dating back to the Grenville age more than one billion years ago. On foot, Shenandoah offers some of the best hiking in the entire country, with

500 miles of trails, including the popular Browns Gap leading to the serene yet picturesque Jones Run and Doyles River waterfalls. Just 75 miles from the bustle of Washington, DC, the park is very popular for camping. In the summer, the days are long and the nights are cool. Visit Shenandoah in mid-August to gaze at the beautiful, starry skies during the annual Night Sky Festival. For those who enjoy staying in the car for long scenic drives or getting out and putting their hiking boots to the test, Shenandoah is the place to go for family vacations, or whenever you need some fresh air.

DECEMBER 2025

NOTES	SUNDAY	MONDAY	TUESDAY
		1 WORLD AIDS DAY	**2**
	7	**8**	**9**
	14	**15**	**16**
	21 HANUKKAH (BEGINS AT SUNDOWN)	**22**	**23**
	28 WINTER SOLSTICE	**29**	**30**

DECEMBER 2025

WEDNESDAY	THURSDAY	FRIDAY	SATURDAY
3	4 ●	5	6
INTERNATIONAL DAY OF PERSONS WITH DISABILITIES			
10	11 ◗	12	13
HUMAN RIGHTS DAY			
17	18 ○	19	20
24	25	26	27
CHRISTMAS EVE	CHRISTMAS DAY	BOXING DAY (UK/CAN/AUS/NZ) FIRST DAY OF KWANZAA	
31			
NEW YEAR'S EVE			

SHENANDOAH NATIONAL PARK

LOCATION: Northern Virginia

SIZE: 199,173 acres

BEST TIME TO VISIT: April through November

FAUNA & FLORA: Shenandoah is classified as Appalachian oak vegetation, with pine dominating in the southwest and hemlock and mosses in the northeast. Find eastern cottontail rabbit, woodchuck, and Carolina Chickadees among dozens of other mammals, birds, reptiles, and more.

ENDANGERED FAUNA & FLORA: The sole endangered species in Shenandoah National Park is the aptly named Shenandoah salamander, which can be found on the park's high-elevation slopes.

MAIN ATTRACTIONS: The 105-mile Skyline Drive stretches the entire length of Shenandoah National Park, situated between Shenandoah Valley and the Piedmont. Experience views of the blue-tinted mountains, dense forests, and fascinating wildlife from your car.

PRIMARY PURPOSE: To preserve the nationally significant natural scenic beauty and designated wilderness of Virginia's Blue Ridge Mountains for public enjoyment, recreation, and inspiration.

DECEMBER

MONDAY WORLD AIDS DAY   1

TUESDAY   2

WEDNESDAY INTERNATIONAL DAY OF PERSONS WITH DISABILITIES   3

THURSDAY ●   4

FRIDAY   5

SATURDAY   6

SUNDAY   7

DECEMBER 2025

MONDAY **8**

TUESDAY **9**

WEDNESDAY HUMAN RIGHTS DAY **10**

THURSDAY ◖ **11**

FRIDAY　　　　　　　　　　　　　　　**12**

SATURDAY　　　　　　　　　　　　　**13**

SUNDAY　HANUKKAH (BEGINS AT SUNDOWN)　　**14**

Follow @shenandoahnps during the fall season to keep up with the color updates of the fall foliage every week, taken from three different areas of the park.

DECEMBER 2025

MONDAY 15

TUESDAY 16

WEDNESDAY 17

THURSDAY 18

FRIDAY ○   **19**

SATURDAY   **20**

SUNDAY WINTER SOLSTICE   **21**

The park is friendly to dogs, except for 10 trails, so leash up your furry sidekicks and bring them along.

DECEMBER 2025

MONDAY   **22**

TUESDAY   **23**

WEDNESDAY CHRISTMAS EVE   **24**

THURSDAY CHRISTMAS DAY   **25**

FRIDAY BOXING DAY (UK/CAN/AUS/NZ)/FIRST DAY OF KWANZAA **26**

SATURDAY **27**

SUNDAY ◗ **28**

Through its artist-in-residence program, the park offers talented artists the opportunity to live and work in the beautiful environment of the Blue Ridge Mountains.

DECEMBER 2025

MONDAY   **29**

TUESDAY   **30**

WEDNESDAY NEW YEAR'S EVE   **31**

THURSDAY (JANUARY) NEW YEAR'S DAY   **1**

NOTES

NOTES

NOTES

NOTES

NOTES

NOTES

NOTES

First published in 2024 by Rock Point, an imprint of The Quarto Group,
142 West 36th Street, 4th Floor, New York, NY 10018, USA
(212) 779-4972 www.Quarto.com

10 9 8 7 6 5 4 3 2 1

ISBN: 978-1-57715-420-4

Group Publisher: Rage Kindelsperger
Editorial Director: Erin Canning
Creative Director: Laura Drew
Managing Editor: Cara Donaldson
Editor: Katelynn Abraham
Editorial Assistant: Zoe Briscoe
Cover and Interior Design: Beth Middleworth

Printed in China

This book provides general information on national parks and their inspirational and holistic benefits. However, it should not be relied upon as recommending or promoting any specific diagnosis or method of treatment for a particular condition, and it is not intended as a substitute for medical advice or for direct diagnosis and treatment of a medical condition by a qualified physician. Readers who have questions about a particular condition, possible treatments for that condition, or possible reactions from the condition or its treatment should consult a physician or other qualified healthcare professional.

All Moon phases shown are for the Eastern Time Zone.